Big Animals in the Sea

Written by Jo Windsor

Rigby

This dolphin is big.

This shark is big.

This octopus is big.

11

This whale is big.

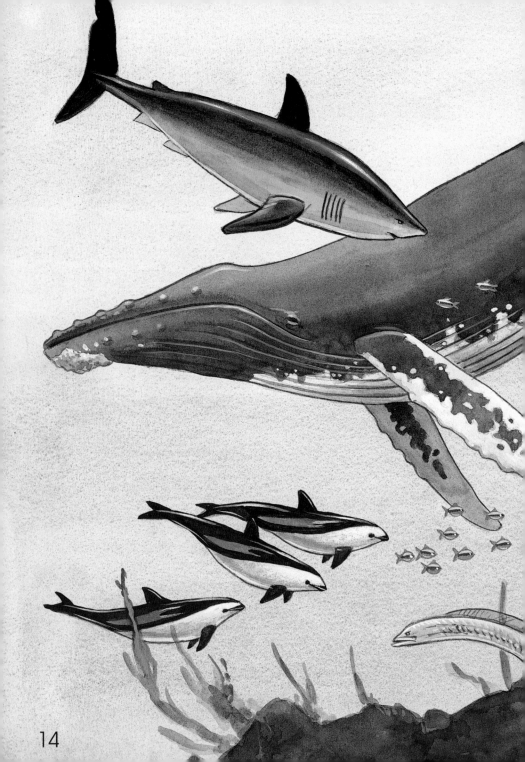

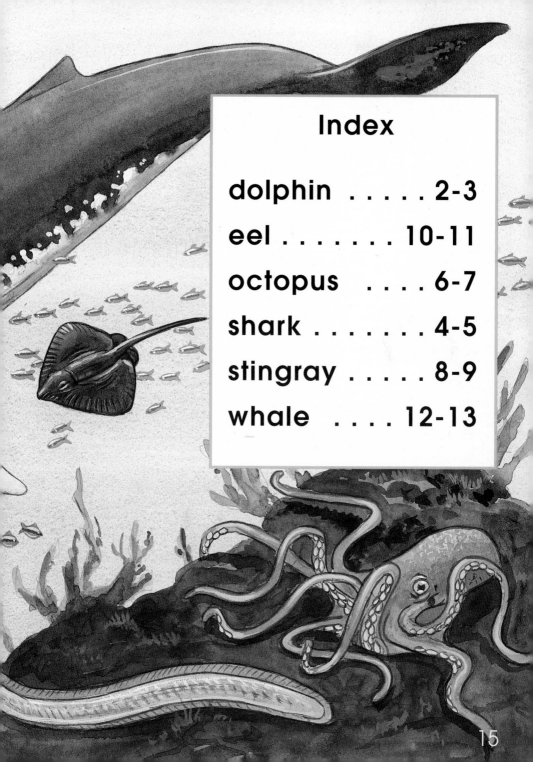

Index

▬ Guide Notes

Title: Big Animals in the Sea

Stage: Emergent – Magenta

Genre: Nonfiction (Expository)

Approach: Guided Reading

Processes: Thinking Critically, Exploring Language, Processing Information

Written and Visual Focus: Photographs (static images), Illustrations, Index, Panel

READING THE TEXT

Tell the children that this book is about some big animals that live in the sea.

Talk to them about what is on the front cover. Read the title and the author.

Focus the children's attention on the index and talk about the animals that are in this book.

"Walk" through the book, focusing on the photographs, and talk about the different animals.

Read the text together.

THINKING CRITICALLY
(sample questions)

- What other things can live in the sea?
- Why do the animals in this book need to live in the sea?

EXPLORING LANGUAGE
(ideas for selection)

Terminology
Title, cover, author, photographs, illustrations

Vocabulary
Interest words: animals, sea, dolphin, whale, shark, octopus, stingray, eel
High-frequency words: this, is